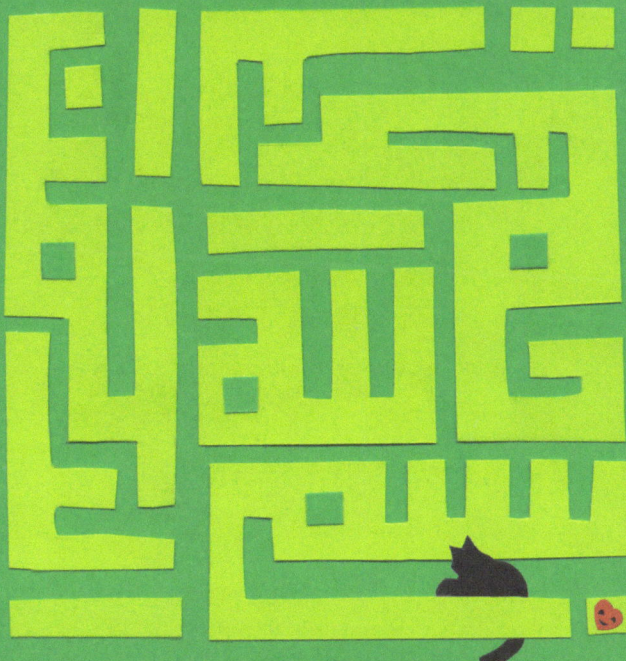

Bismi Allah Ar-Rahman Ar-Rahim.

In the Name of Allah the Most Kind, the Most Caring.

Other Titles By This Author:

My Little Lore of Light
The Light of Muhammad
Links of Light: The Golden Chain
The Story of Moses
Who Are You? A Book of Very Serious Questions
The Animals of Paradise
The Animals of Paradise: Coloring Book
My Little Lore of Light: Coloring Book
Every Day A Thousand Times
Ibrahim Khalil Allah

For the love of the Prophet Muhammad (sall Allahu 'alayhi wa s-sallam) and in gratitude to Mawlana Shaykh Nazim al-Haqqani (qaddas Allahu sirrahu).

And for Haniya, Humayra, Layka, Ishaq, Jacob, Hamza, Ghalib, Khalil, Noura, Karima, Tarik, and Hala.

Printed in the United States of America ISBN 978-0-9913003-7-2

Little Bird Books littlebirdbooksink@gmail.com

As-Salamu 'Alaykum Ya Rasul Allah (sas)

Peace be with you O Messenger of Allah,

(sall Allahu 'alayhi wa s-sallam)

Karima Sperling

I am a rock although some might call me the face of a mountain and some might say a piece of the earth. Some have called me a boulder and some say, just a stone. I don't bother with what others call me because I know that I am one of the precious creations of my Most Loving Lord Who made me.

Allah created me on the day He created the Earth. When He folded up the dry land and drew it out of the sea, He put me high in the sky. I watched as the skirt of earth around me became green with grass and trees, and the dome of sky above me became a reflection of blue. I watched as other creatures slowly appeared. Some burrowed into me and some brushed me with their wings. Some nibbled at the small plants that clung to me and others scratched their hairy backs against me. But we all lived in harmony, which means that together we sang the same song of love to the One Who made us.

One day I noticed a new kind of creature walking on only two legs. He was different than the others. He made a lot of noise and he scraped lines and signs on my sides. But he sang his song of love to his Maker and so I sang along with him.

Over time he changed. His words became harsh and his song became ugly. He even used pieces of me to hurt others. So I stopped listening to him and stopped singing with him. I kept my song a secret to myself.

The years went by. The sun baked me and the cold froze me. The rain rolled off and seeped inside me. Chips fell and became rocks on their own. I grew smaller and older. I felt hollow. Things around me got drier. Plants and animals became fewer and fewer. I fell into a state between waking and sleep and it all passed before me like a dream. I forgot how to speak the words that filled my heart although they still beat a rhythm steadily inside me.

If you are wondering how it is I am speaking to you now, then listen to the story I am about to tell you.

One day I heard something, or maybe I felt something. It was the faraway sweetness of a tune I had almost forgotten. It was a song of love like the songs we used to sing and it was coming from inside me but it wasn't mine. It wasn't a rough rumble like my song. It wasn't a gruff grumble like my song. It was light and yet it had a beauty that trembled and tumbled inside of me. The singer was singing the song perfectly, in just the way it was made to be sung.

I shook off the hazy, dizzy doziness of my long sleep. The voice was coming from the middle of me but it wasn't mine. I listened to it. I loved it. I listened and loved it. I would have loved to listen forever.

I wanted feet to leap with. I wanted hands to hug with. I wanted eyes to see and to shine with. But most of all I wanted a voice to join in the song.

And then it was gone.

I tried to go back to sleep. I rocked myself back and forth. I pretended to be stony and quiet but I only got bolder. I shook the whole mountain with my longing. Who was he and where did he go? Would he ever come back? Oh please, please come back!

And then one day he did.

And this time his song sounded so much clearer and dearer, and so much sweeter - I think because I was wide awake. I believed I would burst into a billion pieces if I couldn't greet him.

Then I felt a cavernous quaking waking within me, a gravelly growling growing inside me. My most Kind, my most Caring Maker had given me a voice again and with it I rang out, I sang out:

"As-salamu 'alaykum ya Rasul Allah!" ["Peace be with you O Messenger of God!"]

And more amazing even than that – the singer heard me! He understood me! And he stopped to answer me!

"Wa 'alaykum as-salam ya khalq Allah." ["And with you be peace O creation of God."]

I was in love.

When his feet touched me I turned to mush. All my hardness softened. All my edges smoothed. All my angles relaxed. I was a pillow under his foot. I was putty in his hands. Whenever he spoke, I listened. Whatever he wanted, I wanted. Wherever he went, I would surely follow.

I was a rock in love.

This went on for years. Sometimes he would spend weeks with me - just the two of us, alone on the mountain, in the sky, singing our songs to the One Who made us both.

Then one night we were joined by a great being of light. My Beloved was afraid but he held his ground and I was proud to be the ground he held. I kept myself steady for him even though I was afraid too. The being of light spoke the words of the One Who made us, words so beautiful they would wring tears from a stone. "Read!" he said, "Read in the Name of your Lord Who created." (76:1).

Once I had heard some mountains say that a long time ago our Maker had written His Word on a stone. Had He chosen me to be a stone like that? Would I have His words written on me? Would I be carried around by beings of light, my sides softly fingered and their tracings sung? Perhaps I was being too bold.

The time my Beloved spent with me became less and less. And after a while he came no more.

I had a voice but there was no one to sing with. I gave salaams but there was no one to return them. I softened but I cushioned no one. So I became hard again. My edges became sharp and my fissures widened. Little by little I broke to bits.

Pieces went tumbling down the mountain like stony tears - bouncing and falling, rolling and rebounding, rocky tears into a valley of sadness. Finally, my heart broke. It rolled slowly down the mountain along the path the Beloved used to take. It was kicked by the sheep browsing on the hillside. Boys tossed it like a ball in their childish games. It was washed down by the rains that flooded the valley. Always rolling down, lower and lower, into a down without end. Tumbled and worn, tiny but alive, I was blown up against a stone wall and there I stopped.

I leaned against the wall, tired and broken. Hardly a rock, just a pebble really, my voice was forgotten. The wall was warm and after some time I realized it was alive. The stones were talking to each other. They were singing their songs of love. They were like me!

I listened shyly. I couldn't speak. These were grand stones, carved, and set one on top of the other for a special purpose. They were straight and great - and I was hardly sand.

The stones were talking about my Beloved! They knew him and they missed him too.

In this place there were two legged creatures who had made him leave. That is why he hadn't come any more to sing with me. They hated him and they hated his song. Can you imagine? They even hated the One Who made them! Certainly even the smallest pebble has more feeling and sense than they. I can tell you that I have never met a rock harder than the hearts that pretended to live inside of them.

The stones in the wall were saying that these hate-full creatures were following after our Beloved to hurt him. What could be done? What could we do? Stone after stone wished to help. "If I were round I would roll all the way to the City of the Beloved and save him." "If I could get free I would fall on the heads of the ones who hate him." But they couldn't because they were heavy and square. They were fixed in place for another purpose.

I listened and felt hopeless. If these great stones could do nothing to help, what could I possibly do? I had wasted all my strength and size in sadness. Just then I heard a new voice, not a rocky voice but a smooth voice like that of the great being of light. I could feel the warmth of him shining on me, blanketing me like the safe, silky night.

He was speaking in a voice that only I could hear. "Little stone," he said "you are round and light and you are free."

Just then a hate-full creature passed by and stepped on me. I clung to his sandal. Holding on as tight as I could, I wiggled and wedged myself between the layers of leather. He mounted his camel and rode off followed by many, many others. We rode and rode but whenever he walked I dug myself into the sandal until I could sense the skin of his foot. I found my edges and made them sharp for him. I gave him a good taste of my hardness and he didn't like it. He looked for me but didn't find me.

For many days I bothered him. Finally, he stopped. Taking a good look, he found me and threw me with an ugly grunt as far away as he could. I flew through the air. I was carried on the wind. Where was I and where was I going? Had I failed completely?

My heart sank.

Tumbled and blown, I sank into a soft dune - a stone, alone among countless others. I lay there motionless, voiceless. Lost.

Then I heard something familiar, something that made my heart beat faster, something that made my insides soften, something that brought my secret voice rushing out of me like a breath of mountain air. In a new, small, high-pitched voice that cracked and broke I heard myself say,

"As-salamu 'alaykum ya Rasul Allah."

And he answered me just as he always had, my Beloved, the one who knows who I am no matter how I look on the outside,

"Wa 'alaykum as-salam ya khalq Allah."

As he held me in his beloved hand, he told me that Allah had chosen me for something special. I was not a great tablet of stone to have His Word written on me. I was not a great block of stone to form the wall of His Holy House. But as a small pebble He still had a use for me.

My Beloved blew on me with his sweetest of breaths and, saying the mighty Words of the One Who made us, he hurled me at His enemies. I became a cloud of dust, a storm of sand, a whirling wind. I blinded the ones who refused to love their Lord. I carried the Word of Allah on the breath of His Prophet and the heartless ones scattered in confusion before me. I was a mighty warrior, a raging wind, an oh so honored grain of sand.

When I finally came to rest I had been carried back to the Beloved, polished and smooth. From then on, sometimes I was the sand on which he placed his holy foot when he stood before his Lord. Sometimes I was the sand on which he placed his blessed face when he bowed before his Lord. But wherever he was, I stayed with him, small and unnoticed by any but him, the dust on his robe, the heart on his sleeve.

And when he became a being of light, I stayed loyally covering what remained in his place, happy always to be near him. And if Allah permits, when my time comes, because all things have a time when they must leave this world, He will make me a speck of light among the galaxies of light that spin around the Beloved and I will be with him for eternity, a heart at peace.

Note to the Reader

Most of the elements of this story are true, only the connections between them are imagined.

According to Sayyidatuna 'Aisha (radhi Allahu 'anha) the Prophet (sall Allahu 'alayhi wa s-sallam) said: "When Jibra'il ('alayhi s-salam) brought me revelation, I would never pass by a rock or a tree except it would say, 'As-salamu 'alaykum ya Rasul Allah.'" Sayyiduna 'Ali (karam Allahu wajh) said: "Whenever I went around the neighborhood of Mecca with the Prophet in the early days of his prophethood, the trees and rocks we encountered would say, 'As-salamu 'alaykum ya Rasul Allah.'"

All of creation has angels assigned to it who are hearing and seeing and protecting. They also have hearts with which to praise their Creator in a dhikr that in this story we call a song. Every particle of creation is a living thing in its own way and worships its Creator with its own heart song. We know this from The Qur'an: "Are you not aware that all things prostrate before Allah, everything in the heavens and on earth, the sun and the moon, and the stars and the mountains, and the trees and the beasts." (22:18).

Even the wind served the prophet Sulayman ('alayhi s-salam). "And unto Sulayman [we made subservient] the wind." (34:12) How can you serve or be obedient to a master if you are not a conscious being? Each creature praises Allah in its own way and the song of the rock is its dhikr.

The Qur'an says: "And yet, after all this, your hearts hardened and became like rocks, or even harder: for, behold, there are rocks from which streams gush forth; and, behold, there are some from which, when they are cleft, water issues; and, behold, there are some that fall down for awe of Allah. And Allah is not unmindful of what you do!" (2:74)

There are many rocks that have the footprints of prophets imbedded in them. There is a footprint of Adam ('alayhi s-salam) on top of a mountain in Sri Lanka. There is the rock with the footprints of Ibrahim ('alayhi s-salam) at the Maqam Ibrahim ('alayhi s-salam) near the Ka'ba. There is a rock with the footprint of the Prophet Muhammad (sall Allahu 'alayhi wa s-sallam) at the maqam of Abu Ayyub al-Ansari (radhi Allahu 'anhu) in Istanbul and another beside the rock under the Dome of the Rock in Jerusalem. It is known that the hard rock became soft to cushion the feet of Allah's prophets and the soft sand became hard to support them.

In every picture there is a black cat because the Prophet (sall Allahu 'alayhi wa s-sallam) loved cats and undoubtedly they loved him. And spiritual beings are known to sometimes take the form of cats or birds. In every part of the story there is a cat watching and guarding and loving - although not necessarily the same cat. Not all people forgot their Lord. There are always some who remember and turn away from fighting for power and keep the peace. The cat keeps them company.

The rock of our story is supposed to be originally from the top of Jabal

Hira, also called Jabal Nur, in which there is a cave where the Prophet (sall Allahu 'alayhi wa s-sallam) used to spend time worshipping Allah and where he received the first revelation. Our storyteller is just one stone from the many that make up the mountain. The Mountain of Light still remains, greeting the pilgrims who come to pray in the place where their Prophet (sall Allahu 'alayhi wa s-salam) prayed and to visit the mountain who was his companion.

The Ka'ba is also made up of special stones taken from Mount Hira and perhaps from other holy mountains around the world. The Black Stone in the eastern corner in particular is actually said to be an angel transformed into a stone by Allah Almighty in order to be a witness to the sincerity of the pilgrims. On Judgment Day it will be given a voice to testify.

It is not surprising that a stone would mourn the absence of the Prophet (sall Allahu 'alayhi wa s-salam). It is recorded that the palm tree trunk that served him as a minbar in his mosque in Medina was heard by the companions to make a noise like the crying of a baby when it was replaced. The Prophet (sall Allahu 'alayhi wa s-sallam) turned and put his arms around it and the crying promptly stopped.

At the battle of Badr the Prophet (sall Allahu 'alayhi wa sallam) scooped up a handful of sand, read on it, and threw it at the enemy. It blinded them and caused confusion. He did this again in the battle of Hunain and it reversed the course of the battles so that the Muslims in both cases were victorious. The force of this breath is shown as the letter 'qaf' which represents the hundredth and secret name of Allah – the word of Allah on the breath of His Prophet (sall Allahu 'alayhi wa s-sallam) that turned simple sand into a whirlwind of divine power.

The journey of the rock is also a child's version of the journey of the self from pride to humbleness, from jaggedness to smoothness, from emptiness to usefulness, from passion to peace.

It is said that if you give salaams to the Prophet (sall Allahu 'alayhi wa s-sallam) you can be sure that he returns them because he is not dead but alive. There is no greater gift to give a child than love for Muhammad Rasul Allah (sall Allahu 'alayhi wa s-sallam).

About the Drawings

The drawings were cut freehand from construction paper with a pair of nail scissors. Everything was cut the actual size you see in the book. Then it was glued onto the background by means of a glue stick as neatly as humanly possible. The aim was to encourage and inspire children with the possibility to make their own pictures.

Jabal Hira or Nur, the Mountain of Light where our story began.

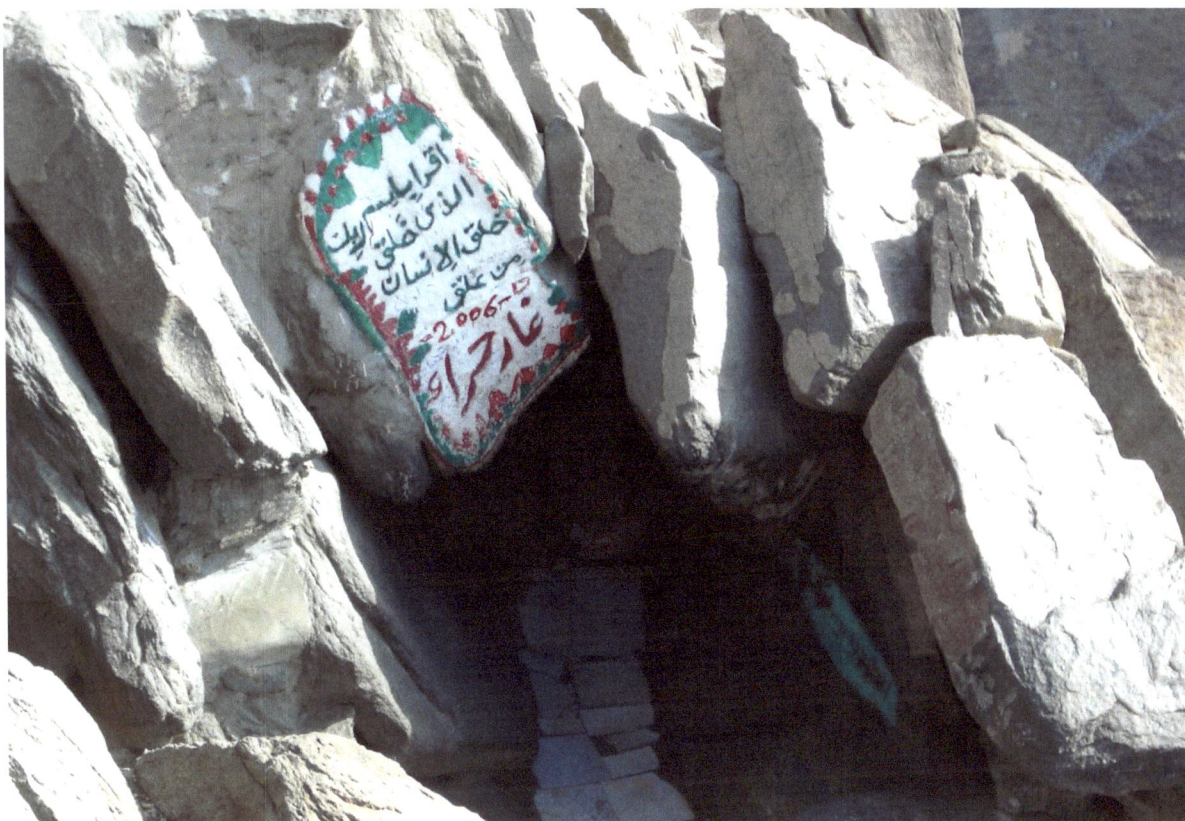

Ghawr Hira, the Cave of Hira in which the Prophet (sas) received the first revelation.

www.ingramcontent.com/pod-product-compliance
Lightning Source LLC
Chambersburg PA
CBHW041550040426
42447CB00002B/120